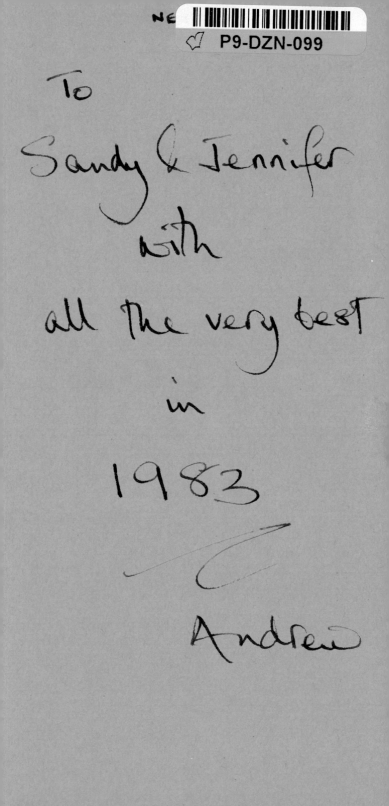

NE

P9-DZN-099

To

Sandy & Jennifer

with

all the very best

in

1983

Andrew

The
Creative
Hostess

BATH
COOKBOOK

We would like to thank all those who have helped us in the preparation of this book, particularly:

Sam Hunt, Curator of Museums
Kenneth Scott, Promotion and Publicity Manager
and all the restaurateurs and chefs listed on page 63 who have so kindly provided us with recipes.

THE BATH CHAIR (previous page) was used as a mode of transport for rich patients when spas, of which Bath was the most famous, were at their height in the nineteenth century.

*"Upon what meat doth this our Caesar feed,
That he is grown so great?"*

Julius Caesar I.ii.148
WILLIAM SHAKESPEARE, 1564–1616

First published 1981 by
Marion Edwards Limited, Fourth Impression, September 1982
10 Barley Mow Passage,
London W4.

ISBN 0 904330 58 3

Printed in England by
T.J. Press (Padstow) Ltd.

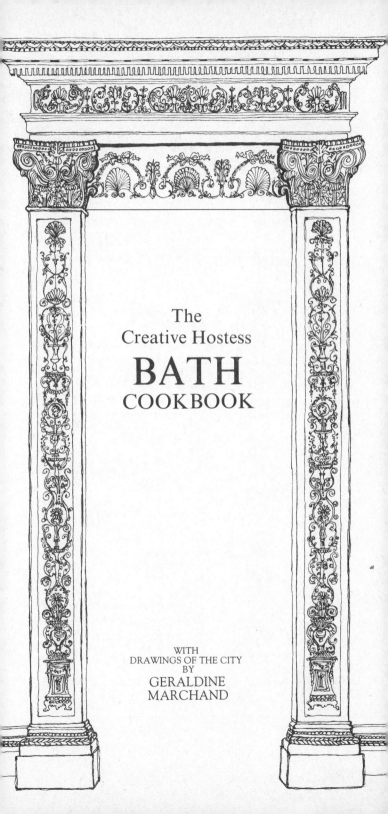

The
Creative Hostess

BATH
COOKBOOK

WITH
DRAWINGS OF THE CITY
BY
GERALDINE
MARCHAND

Introduction

The Romans enjoyed their orgies, and so should you!

Here are some simple but effective ideas for family feasts and feeding friends. The object is to make it easy for you to be one of the revellers at your own dinner table and to throw off your toga/apron before the festivities begin.

But why, you may ask, a Bath Cookbook? Well, first the City lies in an area with a rich culinary heritage, and secondly it has more good restaurants per square mile than anywhere else we know! So this little book offers you the best of both worlds— traditional fare and restaurant favourites, interspersed with charming line drawings. We couldn't resist adding one or two of our favourite ideas too, plus some interesting snippets of information on this beautiful and fascinating City.

Join us on a tour of Bath and share with us some of its best culinary secrets.

Contents

Bath & the Romans

In the year 55 BC Julius Caesar gazed across the seas and decided to invade the small island which we now know as Britain. The Celtic tribes were eventually overwhelmed by the Emperor Claudius in AD 43. Few Romans relished the prospect of being sent to Britain, which they considered a remote outpost of the Empire inhabited only by barbarians. (Some visitors might think things haven't changed much!)

At least the hot springs they found in the West Country at the spot they named Aquae Sulis gave them the opportunity to build a town which would make them feel more at home in an uncivilised country. In its centre, they built a large complex of baths. This was at the site of the hot spring where the native Britons had dedicated a temple to Sul. The Romans, ever practical, simply incorporated their own goddess Minerva and turned it into the temple of Sul Minerva.

In their hey-day, the baths were a popular social centre for the Roman inhabitants of Aquae Sulis, and occupied the sort of place in their lives that a club or sports centre might do today. People met there not only to bathe, but to gossip and discuss business. Here they would meet, talk and socialise, while traders would sell them perfume, wine and honey cakes for their additional enjoyment. They could play sports in an open-air courtyard, then plunge into cold or hot baths, steam away in steam rooms and relax in saunas. Later, they might be massaged by one of the many slaves whose job it was to keep the baths' complex running smoothly. Life for them—shovelling charcoal into the caverns of the hypocausts below—was very different. From information now available it would seem that the baths were a bustling town centre. (A contemporary account by a writer living above public baths at Herculaneum complained bitterly about the noise; he described how there were people singing at the top of their voices, others shouting to be heard above the din, and—on top of all that—tradesmen shouting out their wares.)

After emerging from a refreshing session at the baths, what else would the Roman visitor have seen? Walking along the main street, now Stall and Union Streets, he would have

THE CELTIC SUN GOD, SUL On entering the Roman Baths you are greeted by the magnificent head of Sul. It came from the Roman temple of Sul Minerva and was excavated in 1790. (Some scholars have put forward the theory that the carving of Sul is a representation of King Bladud, legendary founder of Bath, a statue of whom sits over the King's Bath.)

passed buildings made out of the same honey-coloured stone that you see in Bath today.

There were temples, a market and probably a theatre. But it was undoubtedly the baths that made Aquae Sulis famous throughout the Empire.

Situated at the junction of two main roads—the Fosse way, from Exeter to Lincoln, and the road to Londinium, a sort of Roman equivalent of the M4 motorway—the spa attracted all sorts of people. Soldiers would spend their leave there and others came to convalesce. Tombstones discovered on the road to Londinium showed that soldiers and civilians came from as far as Asia and Spain, Gaul, Germany and Belgium.

For four hundred years Aquae Sulis continued to be popular, but by Saxon times it lay in ruins. What led to its demise? The beginning of the end was a rise in sea levels which flooded the baths and silted up the drains. While the baths were collapsing, so was the Empire. No more money was forthcoming to carry out repairs and the baths gradually filled with mud. They lay ignored for centuries, even when a workman in the 18th century came across the bronze head of Minerva. It was left to the Victorians and present-day archaeologists to uncover what you can now see. Even as we write, exciting discoveries are being made as the temple precinct of Minerva is being revealed.

THE ROMAN BATHS

The baths you see today are only a small part of the original complex of swimming pools, steam baths, saunas and hot rooms. These were heated by underfloor hypocausts and covered by huge vaulted roofs.

Nibbles, Dips and Starters

CHEDDAR CHEESE PUFFS

Here is a stunningly simple idea for melt-in-the-mouth nibbles to hand round with drinks.

	Metric	lb/oz	U.S.A.
Instant mashed potato			
Butter	50 g	2 oz	4 tbsp
Flour	50 g	2 oz	$\frac{1}{2}$ cup
Egg	1	1	1
Cheddar cheese	100 g	4 oz	1 cup

1. Make up two servings of instant potato, following the directions on the packet. While the potato is still hot, stir in the butter until it is completely melted.
2. Add the flour and stir well. Break the egg into a bowl and beat well.
3. Grate the cheese and then mix both the egg and the cheese into the potato mixture, and season to taste.
4. Grease a flat baking tray and place small spoonfuls on the tray, leaving a space between each.
5. Bake in a hot oven, 425°F, 220°C, Gas Mark 7 for 15 minutes until the cheese puffs are golden brown.

 Variations Add 2 tsp paprika and 1 tsp dill weed *or* 2 tsp curry powder and 2 tsp minced, dried onion *or* 2 tsp chopped nuts.

"Bachelor's fare; bread and cheese, and kisses."
Polite Conversation
JONATHAN SWIFT, 1667–1745

DUNKING DIPS

Dips as an accompaniment to pre-dinner drinks can remove the need to serve a starter. Surround the dip with raw vegetables, such as sticks of carrots or celery and cauliflower florets, and also with potato crisps and small biscuits.

Herb dip	*Metric*	*lb/oz*	*U.S.A.*
Mayonnaise	300 ml	½ pt	1 cup
Sour cream	300 ml	½ pt	1 cup
Lemon juice	2 tbsp	2 tbsp	3 tbsp
Dried chives	1 tbsp	1 tbsp	2 tbsp
Dill weed	½ tsp	½ tsp	½ tsp
Onion or garlic salt	1 tsp	1 tsp	1 tsp
Paprika	½ tsp	½ tsp	½ tsp

Bacon dip			
Instant bacon pieces			
(such as crumbled Frazzles)	2 tbsp	2 tbsp	3 tbsp
Instant minced onion	1 tbsp	1 tbsp	2 tbsp
Beef or chicken stock			
cube, crumbled	1	1	1
Crushed garlic	½ tsp	½ tsp	½ tsp
Sour cream	300 ml	½ pt	1 cup

To make either dip, mix all the ingredients together in a large bowl. Leave in the refrigerator for 2 hours before serving.

Variations Yogurt or cream cheese may be used instead of mayonnaise or sour cream. If using yogurt, add last (and bit by bit) so that the dip does not become too soft.

SPICY AVOCADO DIP

	Metric	*lb/oz*	*U.S.A.*
Avocado pears	2	2	2
Ground oregano	½ tsp	½ tsp	½ tsp
Pinch of ground cinnamon	1	1	1
Pinch of ground ginger	1	1	1
Mustard powder	½ tsp	½ tsp	½ tsp
Caster sugar	2 tsp	2 tsp	2 tsp
Lemon juice	2 tsp	2 tsp	2 tsp
Mayonnaise	100 ml	6 tbsp	½ cup
Green colouring (optional)			

1. Scoop out the flesh of the pears and place in a bowl or blender.
2. Add the oregano, cinnamon, ginger, mustard, sugar, lemon juice and mayonnaise, and blend or mix thoroughly until you have a smooth purée. Season to taste. A few drops of colouring may be added if liked.

STILTON AND ONION SOUP   *Serves 4*

A speciality of the Beaufort Hotel.

	Metric	lb/oz	U.S.A.
Margarine	100 g	4 oz	$\frac{1}{2}$ cup
Flour	100 g	4 oz	1 cup
Chicken stock	900 ml	1$\frac{1}{2}$ pt	4 cups
Medium onion, chopped	1	1	1
Butter	15 g	$\frac{1}{2}$ oz	1 tbsp
Stilton cheese, crumbled	175 g	6 oz	6 oz
Chopped parsley	1 tbsp	1 tbsp	1 tbsp

1. Melt the margarine, then add the flour and cook carefully to a sandy texture. Add the chicken stock slowly until the velouté has thickened. Cook gently for 20 minutes.
2. Next, sweat the onion in a little butter until cooked but not coloured, then add the cheese. Cook gently for two minutes then drain off any surplus fat.
3. Add the chicken velouté and bring up to simmering point, but do not boil. Season and garnish with parsley.

CURRIED PIPPIN SOUP   *Serves 6*

This is a delicious cold soup to serve in summer.

	Metric	lb/oz	U.S.A.
Cox's Orange Pippin apples	1 kg	2 lb	2 lb
Medium onion	1	1	1
Butter	25 g	1 oz	2 tbsp
Curry powder	1 tbsp	1 tbsp	1$\frac{1}{2}$ tbsp
Chicken stock	1 litre	2 pt	5 cups
Cornflour	1 tbsp	1 tbsp	1$\frac{1}{2}$ tbsp
Lemon juice	1 tbsp	1 tbsp	1$\frac{1}{2}$ tbsp
Single cream	300 ml	$\frac{1}{2}$ pt	1$\frac{1}{4}$ cups
Egg yolks	2	2	2

1. Peel, core and slice the apples and cover with lightly salted water.
2. Chop the onion and cook gently in the butter, but do not allow the onion to brown. When it is transparent, stir in the curry powder, followed by the chicken stock.
3. Mix cornflour with a little cold water. Stir into mixture.
4. Rinse and dry the apples, sprinkle with lemon juice and add to the pan. Simmer until cooked, then sieve or blend.
5. Heat the cream gently until warm then take from the heat and beat in the egg yolks until smooth.
6. Stir in the apple mixture until all the egg and cream mixture is absorbed. Season to taste and chill before serving.

TOMATO AND ORANGE SOUP   *Serves 6*

A delicious light and fruity soup from Clarets Restaurant.

	Metric	lb/oz	U.S.A.
Butter	50 g	2 oz	$\frac{1}{4}$ cup
Onion, finely chopped	1	1	1
Carrot, finely chopped	1	1	1
Flour	50 g	2 oz	$\frac{1}{2}$ cup
Tomato purée	3 tbsp	3 tbsp	4 tbsp
Oranges, finely grated rind and juice	3	3	3
Chicken stock	600 ml	1 pt	$2\frac{1}{2}$ cups
Tomatoes, skinned and de-seeded	1.5 kg	3 lb	3 lb
Garlic, small clove	1	1	1
Sugar	1 tsp	1 tsp	1 tsp
Double cream	150 ml	$\frac{1}{4}$ pt	$\frac{2}{3}$ cup
Sprig of fresh chervil	1	1	1

1. Melt the butter in a heavy saucepan and gently fry the onion and carrot. Add the flour to make a roux and cook gently for 10 minutes.
2. Add tomato purée, orange rind and juice, and stock. Cook until the mixture is smooth and glossy.
3. Put the tomatoes, garlic and sugar into the pan. Season to taste then simmer for about 30 minutes.
4. Place the mixture in a liquidiser then strain. Return to the pan and heat through.
5. Serve with a dash of cream in the centre of each portion and sprinkle chervil on top.

COQUILLES ST JACQUES AU BEURRE BLANC   *Serves 4*

This classic French starter from the Priory may be prepared a little in advance and kept warm in the oven. Serve in scallop shells or ramekins.

	Metric	lb/oz	U.S.A.
Fresh scallops, in $\frac{1}{2}$'' slices	12	12	12
Unsalted butter	200 g	8 oz	1 cup
Shallots, chopped	2	2	2
Bacon rashers, in finely sliced strips	3	3	3
Dry white wine	150 ml	$\frac{1}{4}$ pt	$\frac{2}{3}$ cup
Lemon, juice of	$\frac{1}{2}$	$\frac{1}{2}$	$\frac{1}{2}$
Double cream	1 tbsp	1 tbsp	1 tbsp

1. Place a little of the butter in a large saucepan and fry the shallots and bacon gently. Add the seasoned scallops and cook over a medium heat for 10 minutes.
2. Add the wine and lemon juice, turn up heat and reduce by two-thirds. Gradually stir in remaining butter.
3. Stir in the cream.

14

POPJOY'S OEUFS BENEDICTINE *Serves 6*

	Metric	lb/oz	U.S.A.
Smoked mackerel	225 g	8 oz	8 oz
Lemons, grated rind and juice	2	2	2
Olive oil	150 ml	¼ pt	½ cup
Garlic clove, crushed	1	1	1
Eggs	6	6	6
Vinegar	2 tsp	2 tsp	2 tsp
Hollandaise sauce	6 tbsp	6 tbsp	½ cup

1. Flake the mackerel well, being careful to remove all the skin and bones. Put into a liquidiser with the lemon rind, juice, oil and garlic. Blend to a smooth purée. Season carefully as the fish tends to be salty.
2. Divide the mixture between six ramekins or cocotte dishes. Warm carefully in the oven, covering with foil.
3. When you are ready to eat, poach the eggs in boiling water (you'll need two saucepans), to which a little salt and vinegar have been added, for 2 minutes.
4. Lift out with a strainer spoon and place one in each dish. Spoon over the hollandaise sauce and serve immediately with brown bread and butter.

Hollandaise sauce

	Metric	lb/oz	U.S.A.
White wine vinegar	4 tbsp	4 tbsp	5 tbsp
Lemon juice	1 tsp	1 tsp	1 tsp
Onion, chopped	1 tbsp	1 tbsp	1 tbsp
Bay leaf	1	1	1
Blade of mace	1	1	1
Peppercorns	6	6	6
Egg yolks	3	3	3
Softened butter	125 g	5 oz	⅔ cup
Single cream	2 tbsp	2 tbsp	3 tbsp

1. Boil the vinegar, lemon juice, onion, bay leaf, mace and peppercorns in a small pan until the liquid is reduced to about 1 tablespoon.
2. Beat the yolks in a bowl with a nut of butter and a pinch of salt until light and fluffy.
3. Strain the liquid and add to the yolks.
4. Stand the bowl on top of a pan of boiling water and add the rest of the butter in small pieces, beating continuously until thick and creamy. Stir in cream and season to taste.

 Juliana Popjoy, Beau Nash's last mistress, was a colourful figure; on Nash's death she vowed never to sleep in a bed again and ended her days as a herb gatherer, living in a hollow tree. She is said to haunt the drawing room, dressed in grey.

SPARKLING CREAM MOUSSE   *Serves 4–6*

The sort of recipe we love—it can be made in advance and is sure to impress!

	Metric	lb/oz	U.S.A.
Philadelphia cream cheese	170 g	6 oz	6 oz
Jellied consommé*	1 can	1 can	1 can
Lemon juice	1 tsp	1 tsp	1 tsp
Curry powder, scant tsp	1	1	1
Paprika and parsley to garnish			

1. Reserve 4 tbsp consommé then put the remainder and all other ingredients into a blender and mix until completely smooth.
2. Pour the mixture into individual glasses or small dishes and leave overnight to set.
3. Next morning, heat the reserved consommé until liquid, and allow to cool but not set. Pour a thin layer on top of each mousse and return them to the refrigerator to set.
4. To serve, sprinkle with a little chopped parsley or paprika, and top with a thin, curled slice of lemon.

* If the consommé is not jellied, mix 1 tsp of gelatine with 1 tbsp cold water and heat gently until dissolved, then mix with the consommé and let the mixture get cold before proceeding.

Variation If you do not like the taste of curry (although it is difficult to identify in this dish) try using 1 tbsp sherry or vermouth in place of the lemon juice and curry powder. Season the mixture to taste.

MUSHROOMS IN GARLIC BUTTER   *Serves 6*

An inexpensive, easy and delicious starter.

	Metric	lb/oz	U.S.A.
Mushrooms	600 g	1½ lb	6 cups
Garlic cloves	2	2	2
Parsley heads	3	3	3
Butter	250 g	8 oz	1 cup

1. Choose small button mushrooms, wipe and trim as necessary and dry. Put into a large ovenproof dish.
2. Peel and crush the garlic cloves and chop the parsley finely.
3. Soften the butter by leaving at room temperature and mix in the garlic and parsley. (When the parsley is well distributed the garlic will be, too!)
4. Dot the butter mixture over the mushrooms. Put into a hot oven, 375°F, 190°C, Gas Mark 5, for 10–15 minutes, before serving with crusty French bread.

CHICKEN ROSEMARY   *Serves 4*

A simple but delicious idea for chicken from the Beaujolais
Restaurant.

	Metric	*lb/oz*	*U.S.A.*
Chicken	2 kg	4 lb	4 lb
Oil	2 tbsp	2 tbsp	2 tbsp
Lemons, juice of	2	2	2
Black pepper, coarsely ground			
Rosemary	2 tbsp	2 tbsp	3 tbsp
Pinch of basil	1	1	1
Parsley, chopped	3 tbsp	3 tbsp	4 tbsp

1. Cut the chicken into 8 portions.
2. Brush each portion with a little oil and lemon juice then
   sprinkle with black pepper and coat with rosemary and
   basil.
3. Heat the remaining oil in a pan and sauté the chicken
   portions until they are golden brown.
4. Place the portions in an ovenproof dish and pour the
   remaining lemon juice over the top. Sprinkle with a pinch
   of salt.
5. Bake in a moderate oven at 350°F, 180°C, Gas Mark 4 for
   25 minutes.
6. Serve on a bed of lettuce and sprinkle with chopped
   parsley.

THE HOLE IN THE WALL

This world-famous restaurant is entered through a small
door leading down into a delightfully converted cellar, both
intimate and charming in atmosphere.

POULET CANAILLE
Serves 4–6

Don't be put off by the apparently large quantity of garlic in this excellent recipe from the Hole in the Wall Restaurant. The uncrushed cloves, combined with the butter and oil, impregnate the bird to give it a delicious and subtle flavour.

	Metric	lb/oz	U.S.A.
Two chickens each weighing	1 kg	1¾ lb	1¾ lb
Butter	50 g	2 oz	¼ cup
Olive oil	2 tbsp	2 tbsp	3 tbsp
Large cloves of garlic, peeled	20	20	20

1. Joint and season the chickens. In a heavy bottomed casserole heat butter and oil until very hot. Brown chicken quickly on both sides.
2. Add the peeled garlic, cover the pan and reduce the heat to very low. Cook gently but steadily for 25 minutes turning the pieces at half time and shaking the garlic down to the bottom of the pan.
3. Serve the chicken with all its buttery, garlicky juices, matching up dark and light meat for each helping.
4. Serve with jacket potatoes and a green salad.

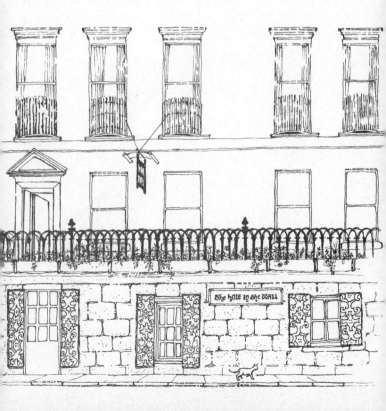

The Hole in the Wall

SCRUMPY CHICKEN BATH STYLE   *Serves 8*

Visitors who decide to have lunch in the Terrace Restaurant
at the Pump Room will discover that it directly overlooks the
Great Bath, and there is a delicious choice of dishes.
Scrumpy Chicken is a very popular one.

	Metric	*lb/oz*	*U.S.A.*
Two chickens each weighing	1.5 kg	3 lb	3 lb
Celery sticks	2	2	2
Carrots	750 g	1½ lb	1½ lb
Onions	500 g	1 lb	1 lb
Mixed herbs	2 tsp	2 tsp	2 tsp
Dry cider or scrumpy	½ litre	1 pt	2½ cups
Chicken stock cube	1	1	1
Butter	125 g	4 oz	½ cup
Flour	125 g	4 oz	1 cup
Pinch of mace	2	2	2
Ham, cubed	500 g	1 lb	1 lb
Apples	1 kg	2 lb	2 lb
Single cream	150 ml	¼ pt	½ cup
Parsley chopped	1 tbsp	1 tbsp	2 tbsp

1. Clean the chickens, cover with foil and roast at 375°F,
   190°C, Gas Mark 5 until just cooked, but not browned.
2. Remove and allow to cool a little before handling. Cut
   each chicken into four
   portions, reserving the
   carcasses to make a stock.
   Put the portions in the refrigerator to cool.
3. Put chicken bones in a
   large pan and add the
   celery, and two carrots
   and two onions, roughly
   chopped. Add the mixed
   herbs and cover with the
   cider. Crumble in the
   stock cube. Bring to the
   boil and simmer for 1
   hour.
4. Remove from heat and
   strain into a fresh pan.
5. Mix together the butter
   and flour and stir small
   nuts of this mixture into
   the stock over a gentle
   heat. Continue to stir the
   sauce until all the butter
   and flour roux has been
   used up and the mixture
   has thickened.

6. Remove from the heat and then stir in the ham and mace. Season to taste.
7. Peel and slice the apples and remaining carrots and onions. Place the chicken in a casserole and cover with the apples, carrots and onions.
8. Pour over the sauce and cover with a lid or foil.
9. Put into the oven and cook at 375°F, 190°C, Gas Mark 5 for one hour.
10. To serve, stir in the cream and sprinkle with parsley.

DUCK WITH CRESCENT PATE TURNOVERS   *Serves 4*
AIGUILLETTES DE CANARD AU CHAUSSON DE SON FOIE

The Chef of the Royal Crescent Hotel has created this lovely combination of duck in a creamy sauce accompanied by duck liver pastry crescents.

	Metric	*lb/oz*	*U.S.A.*
Duckling	1.5 kg	3 lb	3 lb
Brandy	2 tbsp	2 tbsp	2 tbsp
Butter	25 g	1 oz	2 tbsp
Puff pastry	100 g	4 oz	4 oz
Beaten egg for glaze	1	1	1
Carrots, roughly chopped	75 g	3 oz	3 oz
Stick of celery, roughly chopped	1	1	1
Onion, roughly chopped	75 g	3 oz	3 oz
Leeks, roughly chopped	50 g	2 oz	2 oz
Pinch of fresh thyme	1	1	1
Garlic cloves, roughly chopped	2	2	2
Burgundy	$\frac{1}{2}$ bott	$\frac{1}{2}$ bott	$\frac{1}{2}$ bott
Double cream	150 ml	$\frac{1}{4}$ pt	$\frac{1}{2}$ cup

1. Remove the liver from the duck and place in a small bowl with the brandy for approximately six hours.
2. Melt the butter in a shallow but thickly based pan or casserole and cook on all sides to seal in the juices.
3. Place the duck on its side so that the leg is on the bottom of the pan and roast for 15 minutes in a hot oven, 350°F, 180°C, Gas Mark 4. Turn on the other side and roast for a further 15 minutes.
4. Remove the duck and allow to cool until just warm.
5. While the duck is cooling make the Crescent Pâté Turnovers. Put the duck liver and one thigh of the duck into a blender and liquidise. Season well and add the brandy. Leave to stiffen in the refrigerator.
6. Roll out the pastry to 3 mm ($\frac{1}{8}$″) thickness and cut two ovals about 15 cm (6″) in length.

7. Fill the turnovers with the pâté. Brush the outside edge of the pastry with beaten egg and fold over. Brush the top of the pastry with the beaten egg and bake at 350°F, 180°C, Gas Mark 4 for about 20 minutes.
8. Remove the two breasts completely from the carcass and slice them lengthwise into thin slices and place in a fan-like fashion on a serving dish. Chop the carcass and the legs. Place the bones and legs back into the roasting tin with the chopped vegetables, herbs and garlic. Brown all the ingredients lightly and add the wine.
9. Boil down to half the quantity and add the cream. Reduce to the required consistency, season to taste and strain over the sliced duck.

ROAST DUCKLING WITH APPLE AND SULTANA SAUCE
Serves 4

A popular dish at the Beaufort Hotel.

	Metric	lb/oz	U.S.A.
Oven-ready duckling	2 kg	4½ lb	4½ lb
Sultanas	75 g	3 oz	¾ cup
Calvados (apple brandy)	3 tbsp	3 tbsp	3 tbsp
Eating apples	2	2	2
Small onion	1	1	1
Butter	25 g	1 oz	2 tbsp
Double cream	300 ml	½ pt	1¼ cups

1. Put the sultanas to soak in the Calvados.
2. Rub the duckling with salt and pepper inside and out, then roast in a moderate oven, 375°F, 190°C, Gas Mark 5, for about an hour, occasionally basting it and removing any excess fat. To test, stick a fork into the wing and tip up the duck—if any blood comes out, give it another 10 minutes. Cut the duck into quarters and remove excess bones (rib cage, etc.).
3. To make the sauce, first slice, skin and core the apples and chop the onion finely. Sauté the onion in the butter until cooked (but not coloured), then add the apples and fry for a couple of minutes. Add the sultanas and Calvados and reduce the liquid slightly.
4. Finally, add the fresh cream and simmer for a couple of minutes until the sauce thickens (but do not boil as the sauce will curdle). Correct the seasoning and pour over the hot duckling.
Fresh baby carrots, green beans and croquette potatoes go well with this dish.

FAISANT ROTI AUX TROIS PUREES *Serves 4*

Any game is a luxury nowadays and it is well worth the trouble to serve it this way. The purée tartlets can also add a decorative touch to other dishes. This recipe was supplied by the Priory.

	Metric	lb/oz	U.S.A.
Hen pheasants	2	2	2
Vegetable purées	3	3	3
Cream or milk for purées	2 tbsp	2 tbsp	3 tbsp
Flour	100 g	4 oz	1 cup
Butter	50 g	2 oz	$\frac{1}{4}$ cup
Madeira	150 ml	$\frac{1}{4}$ pt	$\frac{2}{3}$ cup
Stock	300 ml	$\frac{1}{2}$ pt	$1\frac{1}{4}$ cups
Unsalted butter	100 g	4 oz	$\frac{1}{2}$ cup

1. Truss and season the pheasants and roast in a hot oven, 375°F, 190°C, Gas Mark 5, for 35 minutes—10 minutes on either side, the remainder on their backs. They should be nicely pink at this stage.
2. While the pheasants are roasting make the vegetable purées. Use vegetables such as swede, turnip or French beans. Cook the vegetables well in boiling salted water, then strain and liquidise with a little double cream or milk.
3. Remove the pheasants from the oven and allow to cool. While they are cooling make the pastry tartlets.
4. Place the flour in a bowl with a pinch of salt. Rub in the butter until the mixture resembles fine breadcrumbs.
5. Mix with a little water to make a firm dough. Roll out the pastry until it is 5 mm ($\frac{1}{4}$'') thick and cut out 12 tartlets. Bake these blind in a fairly hot oven, 375°F, 190°C, Gas Mark 5 for 10 minutes until firm and golden brown.
6. Remove the meat from the bones and keep the meat warm. Break up the carcasses and place in the roasting tin or in a saucepan with the juices from the bird.
7. Add the Madeira and bring to the boil. Boil until the liquid is reduced to a syrup. Add the stock and boil again until the liquid is reduced by half. Remove the carcasses and strain off the juice.
8. Fill the tartlets with the vegetable purées, and place these around the pheasant.
9. Bring the sauce to the boil, add the unsalted butter, whisking vigorously. Season to taste and pour over the pieces of pheasant.

When making flans or tartlets it is always wise to put them in the refrigerator for half an hour before baking. This helps to prevent shrinkage.
To bake blind, prick the pastry with a fork, line with greaseproof paper and half fill with lentils or split peas. Remove for final few minutes of cooking time.

Georgian Bath

Bath's transformation from a provincial town to a fashionable spa began with Queen Anne's visit to the City in 1702. The *beau monde* who spent their winters gambling in London, chose Bath as the "in" place to spend summer.

The gaming tables attracted Beau Nash, who arrived in Bath in 1705 and soon rose to become Master of Ceremonies. He instituted a strict etiquette to public entertainments and it was his influence which persuaded gentlemen not to dance at balls carrying their swords or wearing muddy top boots. He also made sure that important new visitors should not go unnoticed: the Abbey bells would bring the fashionable rushing to see the latest arrival—who would later be presented with a bill for the privilege!

Goldsmith described the ritual of the fashionable visitor at that time (see page 24).

Among popular entertainments was the theatre, and a company performed in the Lower Rooms until a theatre was built in 1749. "The School for Scandal" was written when Sheridan was living in Bath. Indeed, the first rough notes for the dialogue were found under the heading "The Slanderers —a Pump Room scene."

In 1776 Christopher Anstey described the Baths scene:

> *'Twas a glorious sight to behold the fair sex*
> *All wading with gentlemen up to their necks,*
> *And view them so prettily tumble and sprawl*
> *In a great smoking kettle as big as our hall;*
> *And today many persons of rank and condition*
> *Were boil'd by command of an able physician."*

By the end of the 18th century, when Jane Austen came to Bath, the affectations of the fashionable set were frowned upon by more cultured visitors and it is clear that her heroines have a poor opinion of Bath society!

THE ARCADES This maze of small motor-free streets is one of the City's most charming features. It is easy to imagine the arcades populated by the heroes and heroines of all those romantic Regency novels set in Bath!

"From eight until ten in the morning the Company met in the Grand Pump Room to drink the waters, while a band of music enlivened the promenade. At ten they adjourned to the concert breakfast at the public rooms. The morning was employed in chit-chat, and in strolling about the Bowling Green and Parades. Fashion dined at three, at the boarding tables, where sobriety and frugality were strictly enforced.

THE PUMP ROOM

Nobody can visit the Pump Room without being aware of the influence of Beau Nash, who arrived in Bath in 1705 and presided over the City's amusements for fifty years. Under his influence Bath became one of the leading fashionable centres in Georgian times.

Private parties were then unfashionable. At six, the rooms were opened for dancing and play. The M.C. led out the ladies in the order of precedence for the minuet. Tea was then served; country dances succeeded; and the company retired at eleven o'clock. This rule was invariably followed. Even the Princess Amelia was unable to obtain one more dance after that hour.''

BAKED TROUT PARK FARM   _Serves 4_

As served at the Francis Hotel.

	Metric	lb/oz	U.S.A.
Trout, gutted and washed	4	4	4
Cider	600 ml	1 pt	2½ cups
Apples, peeled and chopped	3	3	3
Mushrooms, chopped	350 g	¾ lb	¾ lb
Medium onion, finely chopped	1	1	1
Double cream	150 ml	¼ pt	⅔ cup

1. Place the trout in an ovenproof dish and use enough cider to cover the fish. Add the apples, onion and mushrooms.
2. Cover the dish and cook for 30 minutes at oven 350°F, 180°C, Gas Mark 4, or until the trout are tender and clean when pricked with a skewer. Remove the trout to a serving dish and keep warm.
3. Put the stock into a saucepan and boil rapidly to reduce in quantity. (The apples will turn to a purée.) Remove from the heat and stir in the cream. Season to taste.
4. Spoon some sauce over the trout and serve the rest separately in a sauce boat.

LANSDOWN SALMON TROUT   _Serves 6_

A speciality of the Lansdown Grove Hotel.

	Metric	lb/oz	U.S.A.
One prepared salmon trout*	1¾/2 kg	3/4 lb	3/4 lb
Flour	2 tbsp	2 tbsp	2 tbsp
Butter	250 g	8 oz	1 cup
Dry white wine	300 ml	½ pt	1¼ cups
Fresh chopped tarragon**	1 tbsp	1 tbsp	1 tbsp

1. Season the flour with salt and coarse black pepper and rub all over the trout.
2. Melt the butter in a large pan and make sure the pan is really hot. Place the trout in the pan for a few minutes, turning once, to seal in the juices.
3. Well-grease an oven tray with butter and place the trout on it. Pour butter from the pan over it and also the white wine. Sprinkle with the chopped tarragon.
4. Cover the tin with a lid or foil and bake in the oven for 25–30 minutes at 375°F, 190°C, Gas Mark 5.
5. To serve, slice off the bone and then spoon the juice over the fish.

* Ask your fishmonger to gut, dress and descale the trout for you.
** If using dried herbs, halve the quantity.

TURBOT ROYALE

Turbot was honoured by the Roman Senate and must therefore be considered a fish worthy of being bathed in champagne! As this is rather extravagant for us lesser mortals, we suggest using a sparkling cider or wine.

	Metric	*lb/oz*	*U.S.A.*
Turbot fillets, skinned and boned	4	4	4
Button mushrooms, sliced	125 g	4 oz	1 cup
Onion, medium	1	1	1
Olive oil	2 tbsp	2 tbsp	3 tbsp
Dill weed			
Butter	125 g	4 oz	½ cup
Babycham (2 bottles) or sparkling wine or cider	200 ml	7 fl oz	1 cup
Whipping cream	142 ml	¼ pt	½ cup
Cornflour	1 tbsp	1 tbsp	2 tbsp

1. Wash and slice the mushrooms, and peel and chop the onion finely. Heat the oil in a large frying pan and cook the onion gently until soft and transparent. Do not brown.
2. Add the mushrooms, dill weed and butter. When the butter has melted add the fish fillets, and cook over a gentle heat, turning them over once.
3. Add three-quarters of the wine or cider plus enough water to cover the fillets. Season to taste and continue to simmer until cooked (this will only take a few minutes).
4. Remove the fillets to a preheated dish and keep warm.
5. Add the cream to the liquid in the pan and heat gently but do not boil. Mix the cornflour with a little cold water. Stirring all the time, add to the sauce over a gentle heat until thick and smooth.
6. To serve, add the remaining liquor to the sauce, stir until heated through, and pour over the fillets.

PASTRY PARCEL CHOPS   *Serves 8*

	Metric	*lb/oz*	*U.S.A.*
Pork chops	8	8	8
Onions, finely chopped	2	2	2
Oil for frying			
Tomato purée	1 tbsp	1 tbsp	2 tbsp
Oregano	1 tsp	1 tsp	1 tsp
Cornflour	1 tbsp	1 tbsp	2 tbsp
Red wine	1 glass	1 glass	1 glass
Sugar	1 tbsp	1 tbsp	2 tbsp
Mushrooms	250 g	8 oz	2 cups
Black olives, stoned and chopped	50 g	2 oz	$\frac{1}{4}$ cup
Cream, whipped	150 ml	$\frac{1}{4}$ pt	$\frac{1}{2}$ cup
Frozen puff pastry	1 kg	2 lb	2 lb

1. Grill the chops until lightly cooked, turning once, and set aside to cool.
2. Cook the onions gently in the oil until soft and transparent. Stir in the tomato purée and oregano.
3. Mix the cornflour with a little water to a smooth paste, then stir into the mixture and cook for a further minute.
4. Add the wine and sugar and turn up the heat under the mixture. Stir until it reduces and then toss in the finely sliced mushrooms, stirring until the mixture is a thin paste consistency. Season to taste.
5. Remove from the heat and stir in the olives.
6. Transfer the mixture to a bowl and put into the refrigerator to get completely cold.
7. To assemble the parcels, roll out the pastry (each 1 lb [500 g] packet should be rolled thinly enough to make a square for each of four chops).
8. Mix the cream with the tomato mixture and divide between the eight pieces of pastry, putting a spoonful in the middle of each. Place the chops on top.
9. Dampen the edges of the pastry and fold in to make a parcel. Where the pastry overlaps cut off the trimmings. Push the dampened edges together firmly and turn the chop parcels upside down on to a baking sheet.
10. Using the pastry trimmings, make "leaves" to decorate the top of each parcel.* Brush each parcel with milk and bake in a hot oven, 400°F, 200°C, Gas Mark 6, for about 15–20 minutes.

Variations: For a fruity version try a filling of chopped peaches, nuts and sour cream. **For a hot sauce** replace the cornflour with $\frac{1}{2}$ tbsp cornflour and $\frac{1}{2}$ tbsp curry powder. Substitute apricot jam for the sugar and omit the olives.

* The "parcels" may be prepared to this point the evening before if wrapped and stored in the refrigerator.

LOOKING DOWN
MILSOM STREET

Mentioned as a fashionable
shopping street by Jane Austen, Milsom Street was built in
the 1760's and originally intended for private residences.

This delightful view, showing Old Bond Street on the right,
faces the visitor as he strolls down the hill.

A BATH CHAP is a small but tasty bacon joint—when a
pig's head is quartered, the lower quarters (each with
half the tongue) become Bath chaps. They are usually
sold cured, cooked and breadcrumbed. If bought un-
cooked, soak for several hours then boil until tender.
Coat with browned crumbs and serve cold.

MARVELLOUS MUSTARD

Mustard is very good with all meats, either hot or cold, and
will keep well in the refrigerator. Use mustard powder, or
mustard seed freshly ground, and mix it to a smooth paste
with any of the following:

Cream *or* milk

Strong wine vinegar *or* ale *or* cider

White wine *or* claret

Warm water (never use cold or hot)

Grape juice *or* apple juice

Each has a distinctly different flavour
—experiment to find your particular favourite.

30

THE THEATRICAL BUTTERFLY It is a living legend of the theatre that at the first dress rehearsal of the annual Christmas pantomine a Small Tortoiseshell butterfly appears. This little piece of theatrical magic comes about when the spotlights are turned on. As the curtains are opened the sleeping beauty emerges from her cosy hiding place in the velvet folds, and the legend lives on!

LAMB STEAK BEAU NASH   *Serves 4*

A succulent dish created by the chef of the Beaufort Hotel.

	Metric	lb/oz	U.S.A.
1'' steaks, crosscut from leg of lamb	4	4	4
Red wine	300 ml	½ pt	1¼ cups
Butter	50 g	2 oz	4 tbsp
Bacon rashers, cut into strips	6	6	6
Medium onion, finely chopped	2	2	2
Mushrooms, quartered	75 g	3 oz	1 cup
Flour	1 tbsp	1 tbsp	1 tbsp
Stock	600 ml	1 pt	2½ cups
Redcurrant jelly	100 g	4 oz	⅓ cup
Mint sauce	2 tsp	2 tsp	2 tsp

1. Marinate the lamb steaks in the wine, seasoned with salt and pepper, for 4 hours. Drain off the marinade and set aside.
2. Fry the lamb steaks in the butter for a few minutes on each side to seal in the natural juices. Remove from the pan and place in a large ovenproof dish.
3. Fry the bacon, onions and mushrooms, adding a little more butter if necessary. Add the flour and cook gently until brown in colour, but be careful not to burn.
4. Add the stock slowly until the sauce has thickened, then add the wine from the marinade, the redcurrant jelly and the mint sauce. Simmer for 10 minutes, stirring gently.
5. Pour the sauce over the lamb steaks in the casserole and cook in the oven at 350°F, 180°C, Gas Mark 4 for 35–40 minutes. Serve with new potatoes and beans.

THE THEATRE ROYAL

The theatre was, for many years, the nursery for the London "boards" and many famous actors and actresses, John Kemble and Mrs Siddons among them, played there. It remains a popular attraction to visitor and inhabitant alike.

There has been a theatre in Bath since the 18th century but the present building was opened in 1863. It cost £12,000, this money being raised by subscription after an earlier theatre had been burnt down.

BEEF IN PLUM SAUCE

Serves 6

	Metric	lb/oz	U.S.A.
Braising beef	1 kg	2 lb	2 lb
Onions, sliced	4	4	4
Oil for frying			
Flour	2 tbsp	2 tbsp	3 tbsp
Stout	$\frac{1}{2}$ litre	1 pt	$2\frac{1}{2}$ cups
Plums	500 g	1 lb	1 lb
Sugar	100 g	4 oz	$\frac{1}{2}$ cup

1. Cut the meat into cubes.
2. Fry the onions in a little oil until soft, and put into a large casserole. Add more oil to the pan.
3. Toss the meat in the flour and fry gently until browned all over. Season to taste. Add half the stout and bring to the boil, stirring continuously.
4. Remove from the heat and transfer the mixture to the casserole, mixing the meat and onions together.
5. Wash, halve and stone the plums and put on top of the meat.
6. Bring the remaining stout to the boil, mix in the sugar and pour over the plums.
7. Add enough hot water to barely cover the mixture. Cover and cook for 3 hours at 350°F, 180°C, Gas Mark 4. Halfway through cooking, stir the mixture and add extra salt or sugar to taste.

SAVOURY PUFF FLAN

Serves 4

	Metric	lb/oz	U.S.A.
Water	300 ml	$\frac{1}{2}$ pt	1 cup
Butter	100 g	4 oz	$\frac{1}{2}$ cup
Plain flour	125 g	5 oz	1 cup
Eggs	4	4	4

1. Put the water and butter in a large saucepan and bring to the boil. When the butter has melted add the flour and a pinch of salt and beat until smooth.
2. Add the eggs one at a time, beating after each one until the mixture becomes glossy.
3. Cover the bottom of a greased ovenproof dish with half the mixture, and pipe or spoon the rest around the edges of the dish.
4. Cook at 400°F, 200°C, Gas Mark 6, for 30 minutes, then remove and spoon in the filling.
5. Turn the oven to 450°F, 230°C, Gas Mark 8 and cook for a further 10–15 minutes.

Minced beef filling	*Metric*	*lb/oz*	*U.S.A.*
Butter	25 g	1 oz	2 tbsp
Onion, chopped	1	1	1
Minced beef, cooked	350 g	12 oz	1½ cups
Tomato purée	1 tbsp	1 tbsp	2 tbsp
Worcestershire sauce	1 tsp	1 tsp	1 tsp
Sugar	1 tsp	1 tsp	1 tsp
Cornflour	25 g	1 oz	¼ cup

1. Melt the butter and fry the onion gently until transparent.
2. Add the minced beef, tomato purée, Worcestershire sauce and sugar. Mix together and cook for 2 minutes. Add ¼ pt (145 ml, ½ cup) of hot water to make the gravy.
3. To thicken the mixture, stir in the cornflour dissolved in a little cold water. Season to taste.

VEGETABLE AND CHEESE CASSEROLE   *Serves 6*

Choose vegetables in season to make your own version of this delicious vegetable casserole from Clarets Restaurant.

	Metric	*lb/oz*	*U.S.A.*
Courgettes	250 g	8 oz	8 oz
Butter	1 tbsp	1 tbsp	1 tbsp
Onions	350 g	¾ lb	¾ lb
Carrots	350 g	¾ lb	¾ lb
Celery	250 g	8 oz	8 oz
Leeks	250 g	8 oz	8 oz
Cabbage	250 g	8 oz	8 oz
Sprouts, halved	250 g	8 oz	8 oz
Peppers, finely chopped	250 g	8 oz	8 oz
Mushrooms, quartered	250 g	8 oz	8 oz
Tomatoes	250 g	8 oz	8 oz
Cauliflower florets	250 g	8 oz	8 oz
Cheddar cheese, grated	350 g	¾ lb	¾ lb

1. Prepare all vegetables separately. Slice courgettes ¼'' thick and sprinkle with salt, then cut carrots into small fingers. Skin and de-seed tomatoes. Cut all other vegetables into ½'' squares or equivalent.
2. Melt the butter in a heavy pan and add the onions and carrots. Season. Cover and cook gently for 30 minutes.
3. Add celery and leeks and cook for 10 minutes, then the cabbage and peppers, cooking for a further 5 minutes.
4. Wash the courgettes and add with the mushrooms and tomatoes. After 5 minutes season to taste and add the cauliflower. Cook for 3–4 minutes then divide between individual dishes.
5. Top with cheese and transfer to a hot oven, 350°F, 180°C, Gas Mark 4, for 15 minutes.

Famous Residents

Bath can justly boast more than its fair share of famous residents.

Richard "Beau" Nash (who lived at a mansion in St John's Court, and later, in impecunious times, at Sawclose) and **Dr William Oliver** (who lived in Queen Square, founded the Mineral Water Hospital and invented the famous Bath Oliver biscuit) owe their fame to Bath. Others, already renowned, added their names to the city's residents. **John Wesley,** the Methodist preacher, came to Bath and stayed at 2 Broad Street. He laid the first stone of a Wesleyan Chapel in New King Street in 1780. **Sir William Herschel,** who lived at 19 New King Street, not only conducted the Assembly Rooms Orchestra and played the organ at the Octagon Chapel, but also discovered the planet Uranus.

Dr David Livingstone, who lived at 13 The Circus, is perhaps more famous for being greeted by Stanley in the jungle than for his brave missionary exploits. An explorer of quite another kind, **Sir Isaac Pitman,** is only too well known to young secretaries and journalists struggling to learn the shorthand he invented.

BATH AND THE ARTS

It is easy to see why such a beautiful city has attracted so many writers and artists. Among the most famous are:

Jane Austen (13 Queen Square and 4 Sydney Place) who set her novels, "Northanger Abbey" and "Persuasion" in Bath.

Charles Dickens (35 St James's Square) who set part of "Pickwick Papers" in Bath.

Richard Brinsley Sheridan (9 King Street) who conceived "School for Scandal" in Bath, and who eloped with **Elizabeth Linley** the singer who was then living at 11 Royal Crescent. (It is also interesting to note that while living at 1 Pierrepoint Place the Linley family had employed a young servant girl who later became **Lady Hamilton,** mistress of Nelson.)

Henry Fielding (Widcombe Lodge) based Squire Allworthy in "Tom Jones" on Ralph Allen, who quarried Bath stone and without whom the architect, Wood, might not have built Bath.

Oliver Goldsmith (11 North Parade) who wrote a best-selling biography of Beau Nash.

Sir Walter Scott (6 South Parade), author of "Rob Roy" and "Ivanhoe".

William Wordsworth (9 North Parade) the poet remembered by every school child for his daffodils!

Thomas Gainsborough (17 The Circus) who lived in Bath for sixteen years and painted Elizabeth Linley's portrait several times.

Christopher Anstey (5 Royal Crescent), poet and satirist.

Josiah Wedgwood (30 Gay Street), famous for his pottery.

John Wood, senior (24 Queen Square) and **John Wood, junior** (41 Gay Street) architects of Georgian Bath.

Mrs Sarah Siddons (33 Paragon) who acted at the Theatre Royal in Old Orchard Street.

ROYAL RESIDENTS
Queen Charlotte, wife of George III resided at 93 Sydney Place and held regular receptions in the Pump Room. The less fortunate **Mrs Fitzherbert, Morganatic wife of George IV** had her residence at 10 Queen's Parade, while the **Duke of Clarence, later William IV,** chose 103 Sydney Place. But it was not only British Royalty who were attracted by the City. **Napoleon, later Napoleon III,** resided in Great Pulteney Street.

STATESMEN AND WARLORDS
The tranquil City of Bath must indeed have presented a contrast to the previous areas of activity of the following famous men:

William Wilberforce (36 Great Pulteney Street) famous in England for putting an end to the infamous slave trade.

William Pitt (15 Johnson Street and 8 The Circus), Member of Parliament for Bath and Prime Minister.

Edmund Burke (11 North Parade) statesman.

Admiral Lord Nelson (2 Pierrepoint Street) who spent many holidays here after knowing the City as a child when his father ran a school at 1 New King Street.

General Wolfe (5 Trim Street) of Quebec fame.

Earl Roberts (9 Queens Parade) Field Marshal.

Lord Clive of India (14 The Circus).

Admiral Phillip (19 Bennet Street) founder of Australia.

Major André (22 The Circus) soldier in the American Revolution.

Desserts and Drinks

"Keep songs for after the meal; that is the time for hymns of praise."

SOMERSET APPLE CAKE WITH LEMON SAUCE

Serves 8

This dessert cake recipe from the Terrace Restaurant of the Pump Room is interesting in that it uses no eggs. It is served hot, topped with a tangy lemon custard sauce.

	Metric	lb/oz	U.S.A.
Butter	250 g	8 oz	1 cup
Self-raising flour	500 g	1 lb	4 cups
Apples, diced and cooked	500 g	1 lb	1 lb
Caster sugar	375 g	12 oz	1½ cups
For the sauce:			
Lemons, grated rind and juice	2	2	2
Sugar	1 tbsp	1 tbsp	1 tbsp
Custard powder	1 tbsp	1 tbsp	1 tbsp

1. Rub the butter into the flour.
2. Add the apples and sugar and make into a soft dough. Add a little milk if necessary.
3. Grease two 23 cm (9'') sandwich tins; pour in the mixture.
4. Bake at 350°F, 180°C, Gas Mark 4 for about 1 hour until a skewer inserted in the cake comes out cleanly.
5. To make the sauce, put 575 ml, 1 pt, or 2½ cups of water into a saucepan with the lemon rind and juice. Boil for one minute, add the sugar and stir until dissolved.
6. Mix the custard powder with a little cold water, and pour the lemon water into the custard, stirring all the time.
7. Return the mixture to the saucepan and stir over a gentle heat until the mixture thickens.
8. Pour the sauce over the apple cake and serve hot.

APPLE CHARLOTTE   *Serves 8*

Queen Charlotte visited Bath in 1817.

	Metric	lb/oz	U.S.A.
Cox's Orange Pippin apples	2 kg	4 lb	4 lb
Butter	175 g	6 oz	1 cup
Sugar	225 g	8 oz	1 cup
Lemon, grated rind and juice	1	1	1
Buttered, sliced loaf	1	1	1

1. Peel, core and slice the apples.
2. Melt the butter in a pan and cook the apples over a gentle heat with the sugar and the lemon juice and rind. Stir the apples and watch carefully to see they don't burn.
3. Butter a large pie dish or charlotte tin and line the base and sides completely with buttered slices of bread (buttered side outside). Trim the edges to neaten.
4. Spoon a layer of apples into the base of the dish and then a layer of bread. Repeat until the dish is full, finishing with a layer of bread.
5. Bake in a hot oven at 400°F, 200°C, Mark 6 for about 40 minutes. Turn out of the dish and sprinkle with caster sugar before serving.
6. Serve with cream or ice cream, or a simple jam sauce (heat equal quantities jam and water and stir till boiling).

DEAN'S CREAM TRIFLE   *Serves 6*

A popular dessert from Clarets Restaurant.

	Metric	lb/oz	U.S.A.
Trifle sponges	6	6	6
Raspberry jam	2 tbsp	2 tbsp	3 tbsp
Marmalade	2 tbsp	2 tbsp	3 tbsp
Fresh orange juice	150 ml	¼ pt	⅔ cup
Sweet sherry	150 ml	¼ pt	⅔ cup
Double cream	300 ml	½ pt	1¼ cups
Brandy	2 tbsp	2 tbsp	3 tbsp
Icing sugar	1½ tsp	1½ tsp	1½ tsp
Chocolate, grated	35 ml	1½ oz	1½ oz

1. Cut each sponge in half through the centre and then in half again through the middle. Spread half these pieces with jam and half with marmalade.
2. Using individual glass dishes, place 4 pieces in each, alternating jam and marmalade.
3. Mix the orange and sherry and pour into glasses.
4. Whip the cream, brandy and icing sugar and pipe on top. Chill, and sprinkle with chocolate before serving.

DOT'S TREACLE NUT TART   *Serves 6–8*

Serve hot as a family dessert or cold as a teatime treat.

	Metric	lb/oz	U.S.A.
Plain flour	150 g	6 oz	1½ cups
Margarine or lard	75 g	3 oz	½ cup
Golden syrup	5 tbsp	5 tbsp	7 tbsp
Desiccated coconut	100 g	4 oz	1 cup

1. Put the flour into a bowl with a pinch of salt and rub in the fat until it is like fine breadcrumbs. Using a knife, mix in enough water to make the pastry.
2. Grease an 8″ (20 cm) flan tin and line with the pastry.
3. Put into the refrigerator for 15 minutes, and preheat the oven to 400°F, 200°C, Gas Mark 6.
4. When the pastry is really cold spoon the syrup into the flan case and top with the coconut. Gently press the coconut into the syrup with your fingers so that the whole of the base of the flan is evenly coated with the mixture. Use any pastry trimmings to make a lattice top, twisting the pastry strips for a pretty effect.
5. Bake for 20–25 minutes.

CHEF DUTHIE'S STRAWBERRY FLAN   *Serves 4*

This lovely idea for serving fresh strawberries was given to us by the Chef of the Royal Crescent Hotel.

	Metric	lb/oz	U.S.A.
Unsalted butter	125 g	5 oz	⅔ cup
Caster sugar	50 g	2 oz	4 tbsp
Lemon, juice	2 tsp	2 tsp	2 tsp
Egg, beaten	1	1	1
Plain flour	225 g	8 oz	2 cups
Raspberry jam	2 tbsp	2 tbsp	3 tbsp
15 cm (6″) sponge about			
1.25 cm (½″) thick	1	1	1
Maraschino	6 tbsp	6 tbsp	8 tbsp
Fresh strawberries	225 g	8 oz	8 oz
Apricot jam, sieved	275 g	10 oz	1 cup
Flaked almonds, browned	25 g	1 oz	¼ cup

1. Cream butter and sugar, then add lemon juice and egg. Work in the flour to make a soft dough, then wrap in cling film or greaseproof and refrigerate for 3 hours.
2. Roll the pastry thinly, and line a 15 cm (6″) flan ring. Bake blind in a hot oven, 375°F, 190°C, Gas Mark 5, until golden brown. Cool.
3. Spread a thin layer of raspberry jam on the bottom and top with the sponge, trimming to fit the flan.
4. Sprinkle with maraschino and arrange whole straw-

berries, point upwards, on top. Boil the apricot jam with a little water and coat the strawberries and flan edge evenly, using a pastry brush or spoon.
5. Sprinkle almonds around the outside for decoration.

CLAFOUTIS AUX KIWIS   *Serves 4*

Kiwi fruit are now readily available and are used in this excellent dessert served by the Priory.

	Metric	lb/oz	U.S.A.
Flour	200 g	8 oz	2 cups
Unsalted butter, softened	100 g	4 oz	1 cup
Caster sugar	75 g	3 oz	$\frac{2}{3}$ cup
Small whole eggs	2	2	2
For the filling:			
Kiwi fruit, peeled and sliced	6	6	6
Double cream	300 ml	$\frac{1}{2}$ pt	$1\frac{1}{4}$ cups
Egg yolks	2	2	2
Caster sugar	75 g	3 oz	$\frac{2}{3}$ cup
Kirsch	150 ml	4 fl oz	$\frac{2}{3}$ cup
Icing sugar	4 tbsp	4 tbsp	6 tbsp

1. Make the pastry by sifting the flour into a circle on your work surface or into a bowl, and place the butter in the centre.
2. Mix the sugar, whole eggs and butter gradually into flour, adding 1–2 tbsp water to make a firm dough.
3. Knead lightly and refrigerate for one hour.
4. Roll out the pastry and line a 20 cm (8'') flan tin. Bake blind at 375°F, 190°C, Gas Mark 5 for 25–30 minutes.
5. Place the kiwi fruit in layers, three quarters of the way to the top of the pastry case.
6. Beat together the cream, egg yolks, sugar and kirsch and pour over the kiwi fruit.
7. Bake in a hot oven, 375°F, 190°C, Gas Mark 5, for about 30 minutes or until the mixture is firm.
8. Sieve sugar over the top and place under a **very** hot grill until golden brown and caramelised. Remove and allow the top to harden. Serve at once.

"O noctes cenaeque deum!"
"O nights and feasts of the gods!"
Satires, I.ii.2.
HORACE 65–8 BC

THE ROYAL CRESCENT

Probably the finest Palladian crescent in Europe, with its Ionic columns and a single cornice, the Royal Crescent was built in 1767 by John Wood the younger.

It is composed of thirty houses and is little changed externally from the time when it was built, still being fronted by the same cobblestones over which carriages would rattle.

A modern addition to the houses, one of which is open to the public, is kitchens. The original houses were built without them because the houses were rented for the season, and all food was brought in from outside.

Visitors to Bath may notice that the backs of many of the houses do not live up to their imposing fronts. It has been remarked that much of the City's 18th-century architecture is "Queen Anne in front, and Mary Anne behind".

42

HONEY AND LEMON SYLLABUB — *Serves 4*

Just a few miles from Bath lies the ancient port of Bristol.
Here for centuries ships would come to unload their precious
cargoes of wines and spirits.
Syllabub is an old English recipe which makes the most of
imported Madeira or sherry. Some versions also add brandy.
This recipe comes from the chef of the Beaufort Hotel.

	Metric	lb/oz	U.S.A.
Lemon	1	1	1
Macaroons (page 53)	4	4	4
Madeira	75 ml	$\frac{1}{8}$ pt	$\frac{1}{3}$ cup
Thick honey	100 g	4 oz	$\frac{1}{3}$ cup
Caster sugar	50 g	2 oz	$\frac{1}{4}$ cup
Double cream	450 ml	$\frac{3}{4}$ pt	$1\frac{1}{2}$ cups
Glacé cherries	2	2	2

1. Grate the lemon rind finely (reserving a little for decoration) and squeeze the juice.
2. Break up the macaroons and soak in a little of the Madeira.
3. Beat together the honey, lemon juice, rind, caster sugar and the remainder of the Madeira.
4. Add the double cream and beat until thick.
5. Fold in the macaroons, pour into small glasses, and decorate with a little lemon rind and a cherry half.

REGENCY CHOCOLATE TREAT — *Serves 6–8*

	Metric	lb/oz	U.S.A.
Flour	125 g	4 oz	1 cup
Baking powder	2 tsp	2 tsp	2 tsp
Caster sugar	125 g	4 oz	$\frac{1}{2}$ cup
Butter	45 g	$1\frac{1}{2}$ oz	3 tbsp
Cocoa	$1\frac{1}{4}$ tbsp	$1\frac{1}{4}$ tbsp	$1\frac{1}{2}$ tbsp
Milk	150 ml	$\frac{1}{4}$ pt	$\frac{1}{2}$ cup
Vanilla essence	$\frac{1}{2}$ tsp	$\frac{1}{2}$ tsp	$\frac{1}{2}$ tsp
For the topping:			
Demerara sugar	45 g	$1\frac{1}{2}$ oz	$\frac{1}{4}$ cup
Granulated sugar	60 g	2 oz	$\frac{1}{4}$ cup
Cocoa	$1\frac{1}{4}$ tbsp	$1\frac{1}{4}$ tbsp	$1\frac{1}{2}$ tbsp

1. In a large bowl mix together the flour, with the baking powder and sugar and a pinch of salt.
2. Put the butter and cocoa in a small heavy saucepan and stir over a gentle heat until melted.
3. Stir into the flour and sugar mixture, followed by the milk and vanilla essence. When this is well mixed, pour into a buttered deep pie or soufflé dish.

4. For the topping, sprinkle the brown sugar on top of the mixture followed by the white sugar and the cocoa. Do not stir this into the basic mixture. Finally pour a cup of cold water on top. (At this stage the pudding will look very strange with the cocoa floating on top of the water.)
5. Bake in a low oven, 325°F, 170°C, Gas Mark 3, for 50 minutes. Remove from the oven and allow to cool for an hour before serving. Offer cream separately.

"What use are cartridges in battle?
I always carry chocolate instead."   Arms and the Man
        GEORGE BERNARD SHAW, 1856–1950

CHESTNUT AND CHOCOLATE PUDDING   *Serves 6–8*

Chestnuts were very popular with the Romans.

	Metric	lb/oz	U.S.A.
Chestnut purée	500 g	1 lb	1 lb
Yogurt	150 ml	$\frac{1}{4}$ pt	$\frac{1}{2}$ cup
Dark chocolate	100 g	4 oz	4 oz
Whipping cream	300 ml	$\frac{1}{2}$ pt	$1\frac{1}{4}$ cups

Note: Chestnut purée can be purchased either sweetened or unsweetened. If using the unsweetened variety, add icing sugar to taste.

1. In a double saucepan, or in a basin over hot water, melt the chocolate in a little water. Remove from the heat. Warm the chestnut purée slightly and then mix well with the chocolate. Finally, stir in the yogurt. If using unsweetened purée, sweeten to taste.
2. Pour the mixture into 1 large or 8 small dishes and put into the refrigerator to chill thoroughly.
3. To serve, whip the cream stiffly and pipe on top.

Variation A quick and effective dessert can be made with chestnut purée, cream and meringue baskets.
Whip the cream thickly, and divide between baskets. Sweeten the purée if necessary and then put into an icing bag. Using a writing nozzle, pipe backwards and forwards around the nest, until the top is covered in a bird's-nest effect. Dust with icing sugar.

Frosting Glasses
Any creamy dessert looks especially pretty served in frosted glasses. Whip up an egg white—it does not have to be very thick—and dip the top $\frac{1}{2}$" (1 cm) of each glass first in the egg white and then in the caster sugar. Leave overnight to harden.

MINERVA'S MOUSSE

Serves 6

Fit for the gods, this creamy lime mousse contains hidden rubies and emeralds and has a variety of textures to delight the taste buds.

	Metric	lb/oz	U.S.A.
Lime jelly	1 pkt	1 pkt	1 pkt
Lime or lemon, grated rind and juice	$\frac{1}{2}$	$\frac{1}{2}$	$\frac{1}{2}$
Sugar	1 tbsp	1 tbsp	1 tbsp
Whipping cream	450 ml	$\frac{3}{4}$ pt	$1\frac{1}{2}$ cups
Glacé cherries	20	20	20
Angelica pieces	8	8	8
Marshmallows	12	12	12
Macaroons (page 53) or ratafias	3	3	3
	8	8	8
Chopped almonds	25 g	1 oz	$\frac{1}{2}$ cup

1. Make the jelly as described on the packet but with slightly less water, then stir in the lemon juice, rind and sugar. Place in the refrigerator to cool.
2. Whip the cream until lightly thickened, then put a third in a separate bowl for decoration. Whip this smaller quantity until thick enough to pipe.
3. Place 6 cherries and 2 or 3 pieces of angelica aside for decoration.
4. Cut up the marshmallows and biscuits, and the remaining cherries and angelica—this is easiest with clean kitchen scissors—then mix with the nuts. Stir into the larger quantity of cream.
5. When the jelly is on the point of setting, whisk until frothy then gently fold in the cream mixture. Pour into a glass serving bowl, and put in the refrigerator to set.
6. Halve the reserved cherries and cut the angelica into small "leaves". Decorate with the reserved cream, cherries and angelica.

AMBROSIA SAUCE

This sauce is delicious poured over ice cream. It keeps well and can be re-heated in a few moments.

	Metric	lb/oz	U.S.A.
Butter	175 g	6 oz	$\frac{3}{4}$ cup
Demerara sugar	500 g	1 lb	$2\frac{1}{2}$ cups
Golden syrup	3 tbsp	3 tbsp	4 tbsp
Evaporated milk, 1 can	400 g	14 oz	14 oz

1. Melt the butter gently in a heavy saucepan and stir in the sugar and syrup.

2. Stir the mixture continuously until it is completely smooth and blended making sure you do not allow it to burn.
3. Add the evaporated milk gradually, beating all the time until the mixture is smooth.

Variation Add to the cooked mixture a tablespoon of Cointreau or Grand Marnier, the juice of an orange or lemon, one dozen chopped glacé cherries, and up to 500 g (1 lb) of mixed dried fruit.
Poured over vanilla or chocolate ice cream, this makes a wonderfully rich dessert.

ELDERFLOWER SUMMER "CHAMPAGNE"
Makes 1 gallon

Not alcoholic, but a lovely summer family drink, which sparkles like real champagne!

	Metric	lb/oz	U.S.A.
Elderflower heads	2	2	2
Lemon, grated rind and juice	1	1	1
Sugar	720 g	1½ lb	3 cups
White wine vinegar	2 tbsp	2 tbsp	2 tbsp
Cold water	4.5 ltrs	1 gall	1 gall

1. Take your family into the country and pick the heads of the elderflowers when they are in full bloom. Any not used in the "champagne" will add a lovely flavour to gooseberry fool.
2. Be careful to use only the blooms as the green stems add a bitter flavour. Put them in a large covered container.
3. Over the blossoms sprinkle the lemon rind, juice, sugar and vinegar. Stir all the ingredients lightly. Add the water, stir gently and cover with a lid or plate.
4. Let stand in a cool place for 24 hours.
5. Strain the liquid and pour it into clean, dry bottles. Cork them firmly and store them in a cool place, laid on their sides, for at least two weeks. Be patient, and don't allow the family to open the bottles before the time is up, when the "champagne" will be sparkling and delicious.

"Nulla placere diu nec vivere carmina possunt,
Quae scribuntur aquae potoribus."
"No poems can please for long or live
that are written by water-drinkers."

Epistles I.xix.2.
HORACE 65–8 BC

BAVAROISE

A popular drink invented over 300 years ago, this delicious alcoholic egg noggin deserves to be revived. Try serving it at the end of a dinner party in place of more traditional coffee and liqueurs. The amounts given will be sufficient for 8 small coffee cups or 4 large cups.

Prior to the party you will need to make some sugar syrup. Use a small heavy saucepan and put in it 175 g (6 oz, $\frac{3}{4}$ cup) of sugar and $\frac{1}{2}$ litre (1 pt, $2\frac{1}{2}$ cups) of water. Bring this mixture to the boil, stirring all the time.
When the sugar has dissolved allow the mixture to go on cooking over a gentle heat for 5 mins. Do not transfer to a storage dish until the mixture has cooled.

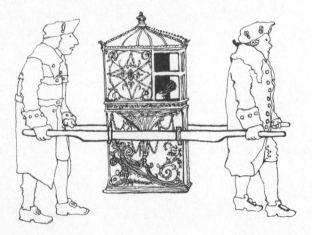

SEDAN CHAIRS You may have noticed that the pavements of Bath are wide, allowing room to turn a sedan chair, which was a popular form of transport. Two good examples may be seen in the Pump Room. (The bearers charged extortionate prices and were wont to shout abuse at any latecomer foolish enough to be returning home on foot!) Lifts were sometimes used to bring chairs to pavement level from basements, and a rare example is to be found in Alfred Street.

THE AMERICAN MUSEUM
Claverton Manor
If time permits, visit this delightful museum to sample Mary Ball Washington's 1784 Gingerbread from Mrs. Small's Kitchen, and see some lovely traditional American quilts. The pattern of this one is very suited to Bath—it is called Caesar's Crown!

To make a coffee Bavaroise
1. Make 450 ml (¾ pt, 1¾ cups) of strong coffee and measure into a saucepan with 300 ml (½ pt, 1¼ cups) of milk. Bring this mixture almost to boiling point then remove from the heat and cover to keep warm.
2. In the top of a double boiler over boiling water (or in a bowl over a saucepan of boiling water) whisk together 4 egg yolks and 50 ml caster sugar (3 tbsp, 3½ USA tbsp). Keep whisking the mixture until the whisk leaves a ribbon across the surface of the mixture.
3. Next add 50 ml (3 tbsp, 3½ USA tbsp) of sugar syrup and the milk and coffee mixture, whisking continuously until heated through.
4. Finally, add 125 ml (4 fl oz, ½ cup) Tia Maria or brandy, pour into coffee cups and serve immediately.

Variations The Georgians were particularly fond of chocolate. A mocha bavaroise may be made with 300 ml (½ pt, 1¼ cups) coffee and 450 ml (¾ pt, 1¾ cups) milk, dissolving 2 tbsp cocoa in the milk.

Another popular Georgian flavour was orange. For this variation use 750 ml (1¼ pt, 3 cups) of milk and no coffee. Add the thinly peeled skin (zest) of an orange to the milk before heating and remove the skin just before stirring the milk into the egg and sugar mixture. Substitute Cointreau or Grand Marnier for the Tia Maria.

LINK SNUFFERS These interesting relics of time gone by can still be seen on Georgian buildings in Bath. They were used for extinguishing lights carried by sedan-chair bearers. This one is in Alfred Street.

MARY BALL WASHINGTON'S GINGERBREAD 1784

This recipe was found in an old worn cookery book. Many of Mary Washington's (mother of the President) descendants have this same recipe.

	Metric	lb/oz	U.S.A.
Butter	100 g	4 oz	½ cup
Dark brown sugar	100 g	4 oz	½ cup
Treacle	150 g	6 oz	½ cup
Golden syrup	150 g	6 oz	½ cup
Warm milk	150 ml	¼ pt	½ cup
Ground ginger	1½ tbsp	1½ tbsp	2 tbsp
Cinnamon	1½ tsp	1½ tsp	1½ tsp
Mace	1 tsp	1 tsp	1 tsp
Nutmeg	1 tsp	1 tsp	1 tsp
Cooking sherry	50 ml	2 fl. oz	¼ cup
Cream of tartar	1 tsp	1 tsp	1 tsp
Plain flour	350 g	12 oz	3 cups
Eggs, well beaten	3	3	3
Orange, grated rind and juice	1	1	1
Sultanas or raisins	175 g	6 oz	1 cup
Bicarbonate of soda	1 tsp	1 tsp	1 tsp

1. Cream butter and sugar and beat well. Add syrups, milk, spices and sherry. Mix very well.
2. Mix cream of tartar with flour and then add alternately with beaten egg to the butter and sugar mixture.
3. Add orange juice and grated rind and raisins.
4. Dissolve the bicarbonate of soda in 2 tbsp warm water and add to the mixture. Stir in thoroughly.
5. Turn into well greased tins and bake for 45–50 minutes at 350°F, 180°C, Gas Mark 4.

This recipe comes from the American Museum at Claverton Manor (see previous page).

In his "Life of Johnson," Boswell recorded meeting his friend Dr Johnson on a visit to Bath in 1776: "We had by ourselves hours of tea drinking and talk." English tea habits do not seem to have changed that much over the years!

A PERFECT "CUPPA"

The English have a reputation for loving their tea and hating that served in many other countries! The teapot is probably the most vital piece of equipment in any English kitchen.

To make a perfect "cuppa", start with cold water and bring to the boil. As the water comes to the boil, pour a little into the teapot, swirl it around until the pot is hot, and then tip it away. Next, put your tea into the teapot. The most often stated quantity is one teaspoon of tea for each person plus one for the pot. For the teaspoonful you could substitute one teabag, but remember that many people like a somewhat weaker brew.

The next most important thing to remember is that the water must be absolutely boiling when it is poured on to the tea. It is this contact of the boiling water with the leaves that enables the tea to infuse fully. This is also why it is important that the teapot is preheated.

Put the lid on the teapot and cover with a cosy. Let it stand for at least three minutes before pouring out. Use a fine strainer. There is much controversy as to whether the milk (*never, never* cream) should be put in the cup before or after the tea. It was, for many years, considered correct to add the milk afterwards so you could most finely gauge the exact amount to be added. It is said that the habit of putting the milk into the cup first originated in Victorian times, when china was precious and it was feared that the heat of the tea going straight into the cup would crack or discolour it.

The flavour of the tea is subtly different whichever way is chosen. Try both and see which you prefer, or serve your tea with freshly squeezed lemon. The above instructions refer to Indian tea. China tea, which is delicately perfumed, is never made as strongly as Indian tea and is most often served unstrained without the addition of milk or lemon.

SILHOUETTES Very popular in Georgian times, silhouettes were no doubt regarded by the visitor to Bath as the equivalent to today's holiday snapshots.

SALLY LUNN'S

"No more I heed the Muffin's zest,
The Yorkshire cake or bun,
Sweet muse of poetry, teach me how
To make a Sally Lunn."

In Lilliput Alley you will find the City's oldest house, built in 1482 and occupied by the Dukes of Kingston.

It was in 1680 that Sally Lunn started her bakery here, and it survives as a popular teashop to this day. The original Sally Lunn teacakes, made to a secret recipe which accompanies the deeds of the house, are still being served—hot and generally oozing with butter—to the wandering visitor. The recipe below produces a very similar result.

The bakery still contains the original ovens and the foot trough in which large quantities of dough were pounded. We are assured that while the original recipe is followed most carefully, this method of kneading is definitely omitted!

SALLY LUNN TEACAKES

	Metric	lb/oz	U.S.A.
Milk	225 ml	8 fl. oz	1 cup
Butter	30 g	1 oz	2 tbsp
Dried yeast	25 g	$\frac{3}{4}$ oz	$1\frac{1}{2}$ tbsp
Sugar	50 g	2 oz	4 tbsp
Eggs, beaten	2	2	2
Plain flour	350 g	12 oz	$2\frac{1}{2}$ cups
Sugar and milk for glaze			

1. Well grease a baking sheet or two round cake tins, then leave in a warm place.
2. Dissolve the butter and sugar (less 1 tsp) in the milk, heating gently—do not boil. Remove from the heat.
3. Mix the yeast and 1 tsp sugar together to a cream and add this to the warm (not hot) milk with the beaten egg. Let it stand for 1 hour.
4. Sift the flour and salt into a large bowl, make a well in the centre and add the strained liquid. Mix well to a soft dough.
5. Knead lightly for two minutes on a floured board. Cut the dough into equal pieces and shape each piece into a round. Transfer to the greased sheet or tins.
6. Cover with a warmed cloth and leave in a warm place to rise for 35 minutes or until the dough has doubled in size.
7. Bake for 20–25 minutes at 425°F, 210°C, Gas Mark 7.
8. Brush the top with a tablespoonful of sugar mixed with 1 tablespoonful of milk and pop back into the oven for a few minutes to dry the glaze.

The resulting bun is not in itself as sweet as a modern teacake and is often eaten warm, spread with butter sprinkled with brown sugar.

BATH BUNS

One of the nicest things about Bath Buns is their sugar topping. Nib sugar is obtainable in Bath, but alternatively you can, of course, use granulated sugar. This recipe comes from the Pump Room Restaurant.

	Metric	lb/oz	U.S.A.
Yeast	30 g	1 oz	1 pkg
Sugar	30 g	1 oz	2 tbsp
Flour	30 g	1 oz	$\frac{1}{4}$ cup
Warm milk	150 ml	$\frac{1}{4}$ pt	$\frac{1}{2}$ cup
Flour	500 g	1 lb	4 cups
Melted butter	60 g	2 oz	4 tbsp
Sugar	60 g	2 oz	$\frac{1}{4}$ cup
Warm milk	60 ml	4 tbsp	5 tbsp
Eggs	4	4	4
Mixed peel	15 g	$\frac{1}{2}$ oz	2 tbsp
Currants	30 g	1 oz	3 tbsp

Beaten egg and sugar
   for topping

1. Mix together the yeast and the sugar and stir, with 30 g (1 oz, $\frac{1}{4}$ cup) flour, into the milk. Put aside, in a warm place, and leave until it becomes frothy.
2. Warm the remaining flour and mix in a pinch of salt. Stir in the melted butter and sugar.
3. Make a well in the centre and pour in the creamed yeast. Add the extra milk and eggs and mix to a light dough. Leave in a warm place to rise till double its size.
4. Add the peel and currants to the dough at this stage and knead lightly.
5. Divide the dough into buns, and place fairly close together on a lightly greased baking tray. Leave to prove in a warm place for $\frac{1}{2} - \frac{3}{4}$ hour.
6. Brush with beaten egg, and sprinkle sugar on top.
7. Bake in a hot oven, 425°F, 220°C, Gas Mark 7, for 15–20 minutes.
8. To make a glaze, boil together 2 tbsp each water and sugar until syrupy but not thick. Brush over the buns immediately they come out of the oven.

For those left-over Bath Buns: Pump Room Pudding
1. Cut the Bath Buns in half and spread with butter and apricot jam.
2. Arrange in the bottom of a baking dish.
3. Make an egg custard by stirring three eggs and 1 tbsp sugar into 575 ml, 1 pt or $2\frac{1}{2}$ cups of hot milk and bring to the boil.
4. Strain over the buns and cook at 350°F, 180°C, Gas Mark 4 for about 35 minutes, or until the custard is set.

"ZUMERSET" ROCK CAKES

Another speciality of the Pump Room Restaurant is their Rock Cakes. These are very popular at coffee time with locals and visitors alike, but be warned—they are a meal in themselves!

	Metric	lb/oz	U.S.A.
Plain flour	500 g	1 lb	4 cups
Baking powder	30 g	1 oz	$\frac{1}{4}$ cup
Butter	125 g	4 oz	$\frac{1}{2}$ cup
Caster sugar	120 g	4 oz	$\frac{1}{2}$ cup
Egg	1	1	1
Currants	65 g	2 oz	$\frac{1}{2}$ cup
Sultanas	30 g	1 oz	$\frac{1}{4}$ cup
Mixed peel	30 g	1 oz	$\frac{1}{4}$ cup
Apples, cooked and sliced	120 g	4 oz	1 cup
Peel of $\frac{1}{2}$ lemon, finely grated			
Milk to mix			
Beaten egg for glaze	1	1	1
Granulated sugar	2 tbsp	2 tbsp	3 tbsp

1. Sift the flour and baking powder. Rub in the butter.
2. Add the sugar and egg and beat well.
3. Stir in the currants, sultanas, mixed peel, apples and lemon zest.
4. Add enough milk to make a very slightly wet dough.
5. Spoon the mixture—to make 7 cakes—on to a greased baking tray. Roughen with a fork.
6. Brush with egg, sprinkle with sugar and bake for 10–15 minutes at 420°F, 210°C, Gas Mark 7 until golden brown.

Bath was in Somerset until 1974, when it became part of the new county of Avon.

MACAROONS

These light and crispy almond biscuits make a lovely accompaniment to any creamy dessert.

	Metric	lb/oz	U.S.A.
Ground almonds	50 g	2 oz	$\frac{1}{2}$ cup
Ground rice	1 tsp	1 tsp	1 tsp
Caster sugar	100 g	4 oz	$\frac{1}{2}$ cup
Almond essence	3 drops	3 drops	3 drops
Egg white, large	1	1	1
Blanched almonds	25 g	1 oz	3 tbsp
Rice paper			

1. Mix together the ground almonds, rice and sugar.

Continued overleaf

2. Stir in the almond essence and egg white. Mix this to a paste. It should be fairly stiff. Add a small amount of water if necessary. Beat for 5 minutes.
3. Put the rice paper on baking trays and put teaspoons of the mixture on the paper, allowing room for spreading.
4. Brush with a little cold water and place half a blanched almond in the centre of each macaroon.
5. Bake for 20–25 minutes at 325°F, 170°C, Gas Mark 3.

JUPITER'S CLOUD CAKE

The Romans were very fond of walnuts and called them Jupiter's acorns. This recipe combines the best of old and new: walnuts from Italy and frosting from America.

	Metric	lb/oz	U.S.A.
Butter, cut in pieces	175 g	6 oz	$\frac{3}{4}$ cup
Caster sugar	175 g	6 oz	$\frac{3}{4}$ cup
Eggs	3	3	3
Self-raising flour	175 g	6 oz	1$\frac{1}{2}$ cups**
Walnuts, chopped	175 g	6 oz	1$\frac{1}{2}$ cups
Coffee essence*	1$\frac{1}{2}$ tbsp	1$\frac{1}{2}$ tbsp	1$\frac{1}{2}$ tbsp

1. Cream the butter and sugar until light and fluffy.
2. Beat in the eggs one at a time, beating in a little flour between each egg.
3. Fold in the remaining flour, walnuts and coffee essence.
4. Spoon the mixture into two well greased sandwich tins.
5. Bake for 25–30 minutes at 350°F, 180°C, Gas Mark 4, until golden brown. Turn out on to a wire cooling rack.

* Use Camp or strongly made real or instant coffee.
** 1$\frac{1}{2}$ cups flour and 2 tsp baking soda.

American Frosting

	Metric	lb/oz	U.S.A.
Egg whites	2	2	2
Granulated sugar	500 g	1 lb	2 cups
Water	150 ml	$\frac{1}{4}$ pt	$\frac{1}{2}$ cup
Walnut halves	10	10	10

1. Place the egg whites in a clean, dry bowl and whisk until they are very stiff.
2. Make a syrup by dissolving the sugar in the water. Stir over a low heat and when all the sugar is dissolved turn up the heat and bring to the boil. Keep the mixture boiling until a little dropped into cold water forms a soft ball.
3. Continue whisking the egg whites and gradually add the boiling syrup. Whisk until the mixture is thick and will coat the back of a wooden spoon.
4. Sandwich the two layers together with some frosting. Spread the rest over the gâteau and roughen with a knife. Decorate the top with walnuts.

PARADE GARDENS

Walk round the back of Bath Abbey and you will discover Parade Gardens.

FROSTING FLOWERS

For these very attractive cake decorations you will need edible flower heads. Primroses or hyacinths are ideal. Collect the flowers while in full bloom. Wash them if necessary and allow to dry completely.

You will need 1 tbsp rock gum arabic and 1 tbsp rose-water —both these can be purchased from a good chemist—some caster sugar and a paintbrush. Crush the gum arabic in a pestle and mortar or with a rolling pin.

Stir the mixture gently in a basin standing over a saucepan of hot water until the gum arabic is completely dissolved in the rose water. Set on one side until warm. Paint the flower heads carefully, coating all the petals, then dust with sugar and leave to dry on greaseproof paper. When completely dry, place in an airtight tin to keep indefinitely.

A CITY OF FLOWERS Bath is the only town to have twice won the Entente Florale, *awarded to the supreme floral city of Europe.*

FLORENTINES

The 19th-century writer, William Savage Landor, said there were only two places he could live: Bath because it was so much like Florence and Florence because it was so much like Bath!

	Metric	lb/oz	U.S.A.
Butter	100 g	4 oz	$\frac{1}{2}$ cup
Caster sugar	100 g	4 oz	$\frac{1}{2}$ cup
Candied peel, chopped	100 g	4 oz	$\frac{3}{4}$ cup
Almonds, chopped	150 g	6 oz	$1\frac{1}{4}$ cups
Glacé cherries, chopped	6	6	6
Whipping cream	2 tbsp	2 tbsp	3 tbsp
Chocolate	100 g	4 oz	4 oz

1. Melt the butter in a saucepan, add the sugar and bring to the boil over a gentle heat, stirring all the time.
2. Remove from the heat, stir in the peel, almonds and cherries, and mix well.
3. Set the oven at 350°F, 180°C, Gas Mark 4.
4. Whip the cream until it just holds its shape and then fold into the mixture. Put into the refrigerator to cool.
5. Well grease a baking tray with a little melted butter and then drop spoonfuls of the mixture on to the tray, leaving plenty of space for the biscuits to spread.

6. Leave in a cool place or the refrigerator for 30 minutes to set before baking. Bake for 4 minutes.

7. Remove from the oven and use a palette knife to ease the Florentine edges back into shape and to stop them spreading further. Put back into the oven for a few more minutes.

8. When cooked, remove from the oven and let them set slightly before easing from the tray with a knife and leaving to cool.

9. Melt the chocolate in a basin over a pan of hot water, then remove and allow to cool until it becomes thick. Stir gently to keep the chocolate looking glossy.

10. Spread the flat side of each Florentine with chocolate and use a fork to make wavy lines across the chocolate. Leave to set.

PULTENEY BRIDGE

This was built in 1770 for William Pulteney by the famous architect Robert Adam. It is his only work in Bath. It spans the River Avon and puts one in mind of the Ponte Vecchio in Florence with its small shops lining both sides.

In summer the weir just below the bridge, which is a replacement of an historic Abbey weir, provides a favourite playground for canoeists and bathers.

THE BATH ABBEY ANGELS

Look again at the imposing entrance to Bath Abbey, and you
will see Jacob's ladder ascending and descending between
an olive tree and a crown on either side of the door. As can
be seen, not all the angels are making it to the top—some are
tumbling down! The olive tree and the crown are a subtle
reference to Oliver King—Bishop of Bath and Wells—who in
1499 had a dream which inspired him to build a new Abbey.

ANGEL CAKE

True angel cake is so named because of its lightness which
it owes entirely to its stiffly beaten egg whites. It contains no
fat or baking powder. Sift flour *before* measuring.

	Metric	lb/oz	U.S.A.
Egg whites	8	8	8
Flour	100 g	3½ oz	¾ cup
Caster sugar	225 g	8 oz	1 cup
Cream of tartar, scant teaspoonful	1	1	1
Vanilla essence	4 drops	4 drops	4 drops
Almond essence	2 drops	2 drops	2 drops

1. If the eggs have been in the refrigerator, separate the
   whites and leave them in the kitchen in a bowl until they
   have warmed to room temperature.
2. Turn on the oven to 375°F, 190°C, Gas Mark 5.
3. Mix the flour and half the sugar together. To make the
   cake light it should be *very* well sifted, so sift it together
   three or four times.
4. Add the cream of tartar and a pinch of salt to the egg
   whites and beat until starting to form peaks. Gradually
   add the remaining sugar to the egg whites, beating continuously until the mixture forms stiff peaks.
5. Fold the vanilla and almond essence gently into the egg
   whites. Sift the flour and sugar into the mixture, bit by bit,
   gently folding in after each addition until the flour and
   egg whites are blended together.
6. Using a spatula, turn the mixture into a 20 cm (8") cake
   tin (this should not be greased but the base may be lined
   with greaseproof paper). Making sure you have no large
   air pockets in the mixture, smooth the top with the
   spatula.
7. Bake fairly low in the oven for about 30 minutes or until
   it springs back when pressed gently with the fingers.
8. Remove from the oven and leave until completely cold
   before taking out of the tin. Loosen with the spatula
   carefully before removing.
9. This cake may be served plain or topped with the frosting
   on page 54.

"Man did eat Angels' food."   Psalm 28, v. 25

TOFFEE APPLES
Makes 6

	Metric	lb/oz	U.S.A.
Sweet dessert apples	6	6	6
Demerara sugar	450 g	1 lb	4 cups
Butter	50 g	2 oz	4 tbsp
Vinegar	2 tsp	2 tsp	2 tsp
Water	150 ml	$\frac{1}{4}$ pt	$\frac{2}{3}$ cup
Golden syrup	1 tbsp	1 tbsp	$1\frac{1}{2}$ tbsp

1. Wash the apples and push wooden sticks firmly into the cores.
2. Put all the ingredients except the apples into a heavy saucepan. Heat gently until dissolved and then boil rapidly for five minutes, stirring to prevent sticking.
3. Test the syrup by dropping a very little into some cold water on a saucer to see if it will form a hard ball. If necessary, continue boiling until this hard ball stage has been reached.

4. Well grease a flat baking tray.
5. Dip the apples into the toffee, twirl around for a few seconds, then place on the baking tray to cool.
6. Any left-over syrup can be poured into a greased baking tin and cut into squares of toffee.

MAGIC ORANGES
Makes 32 segments

There is nothing like a little bit of magic at a children's party. See if they can guess how the orange got into these magic segments.

1. You will need 8 medium oranges and 1 packet of orange jelly.
2. Cut each orange in half with a sharp knife and then squeeze out all the juice, being careful to keep the orange halves intact.
3. Measure the juice and, if necessary, add cold water to make up the jelly—follow the instructions on the packet, but use three-quarters of the liquid quantity stated. Place in the refrigerator.
4. Gently remove all the skin and pith from the inside of the orange halves, and place each one firmly on a cup.
5. When the jelly is cool but not set, pour into the oranges.
6. When set, cut each half into two.

Index

Popjoy's oeufs Benedictine appeared in "Country Cuisine" by Elizabeth Kent, published by Sidgwick & Jackson.
Illustrations on pages 49 and 60 are reproduced from "Silhouettes", and on 1, 2, 18, 27, 32, and 45 from "Food and Drink", published by Dover Publications, New York.

MEASURES & CONVERSIONS

Ingredients are given in metric, Imperial and American measures. **Use measures from one column only.**
Teaspoon and tablespoon measures in the metric column correspond to 5 ml and 15 ml respectively.
The table below will help our American readers.

English	American
Single cream	Light cream
Double cream	Heavy cream
Caster sugar	Fine granulated sugar
Demerara sugar	Soft, light brown sugar
Icing sugar	Confectioners' sugar
Golden syrup	Light corn syrup
Cornflour	Cornstarch
Desiccated coconut	Shredded coconut
Plain chocolate	Semi-sweet chocolate
Bicarbonate of soda	Baking soda

RESTAURANTS & HOTELS

We would like to thank the following for their help and generosity in giving us the recipes listed below.

THE BEAUFORT HOTEL   63411
Chef: Kean Maslen
   Stilton and onion soup, 12
   Roast duckling with apple and sultana sauce, 20
   Lamb steak Beau Nash, 30
   Honey and lemon syllabub, 42

BEAUJOLAIS RESTAURANT   23417
Chef: Philippe Wall
   Chicken baked with rosemary, 16

CLARETS   66688
Chef: David Tearle
   Tomato and orange soup with fresh chervil, 13
   Vegetable and cheese casserole, 33
   Dean's cream trifle, 37

THE FRANCIS HOTEL   24257
Chef: R. Reid
   Baked trout Park Farm, 26

THE HOLE IN THE WALL   25242
Chef: A. T. Cumming
   Poulet canaille, 17

THE LANSDOWN GROVE HOTEL   315891
Chef: Peter Viner
   Baked salmon trout, 26

POPJOY'S RESTAURANT   60494
   Oeufs Benedictine, 14

THE PRIORY   331922
   Coquilles St. Jacques au beurre blanc, 13
   Faisant rôti aux trois purées, 21
   Clafoutis aux kiwis, 39

THE PUMP ROOM AND TERRACE RESTAURANT   61111
Chef: David Cox
   Scrumpy chicken Bath style, 18
   Somerset apple cake with lemon sauce, 36
   Bath buns, 52
   "Zumerset" rock cakes, 53

THE ROYAL CRESCENT HOTEL   319090
Chef: Raymond Duthie
   Aiguillettes de canard au chausson de son foie, 19
   Chef Duthie's strawberry flan, 38

We would also like to thank THE AMERICAN MUSEUM for their Gingerbread (p. 48) and SALLY LUNN'S (p. 51).

FAREWELL   *"The cook was a good cook,*
as cooks go;
and as cooks go
he went."

...but we shall be back with more culinary rambles. Look out for other books in this series on your travels.